The Soul That Speaks

JaVonte Williams

BookLeaf
Publishing

The Soul That Speaks © 2022 JaVonte
Williams

All rights reserved.

Presentation by *BookLeaf Publishing*

Web: www.bookleafpub.com

E-mail: info@bookleafpub.com

ISBN: 978-93-95950-19-0

First edition 2022

ACKNOWLEDGEMENT

I would like to acknowledge Chris Rice a.k.a
DeepSeaRice and Lance G. Newman a.k.a
Mr.SpreadLove. As they have impacted the
poetry scene in the Louisville community.
Creating platforms for individuals like myself to
showcase their passion.

Don't Judge Me

I ask, could you please never mistake my
physical presence for a lack of intelligence.
You just have seemed to catch me
in my natural element.
Your pre-assembled thoughts can be left in that
stereotypical vault you seem to call your mind.
Because you see my physical presence,
does not determine my capabilities.
That succeed far beyond your measures.
The color of my skin does not dictate the rooms
that I should fit in.
My mind is so diverse that it can adapt to any
situation my life requires.
It's sad to think that you only envision, good out
me if there's a tie around my neck.
But your reality hopes that I allow it to be a
noose that will slowly kill me.
For stepping into a place where society,
does not feel like I belong.
So, my friend, I'm here to tell you
that you are wrong.
My physical presence will grab hold of that tie,
and use it as a rope to help me
in my climb to the top.
Your preconceived notions will be
treated like a piñata and busted wide open

by my capabilities.
Leaving you feeling inferior in my presence.
As I expose you to my intelligence that has
catapulted me to the highest degree that,
not even college could grant me.

So, I ask of you again please
don't be quick to judge me.

Silence

Silence…

The loudest form of communication.
The lack of words breaks more bones,
than sticks and stones.
Crumbling souls like hearts
that feed off words of affirmation.
It's ironic that something that has no noise.
Speaks volumes louder than the cries,
of babies who lack attention.
But let me not forget to mention.
Silence can be a suspect and a victim.
Causing so much hurt to those who,
seek any form of retaliation.
While simultaneously bottling up the words.
Of an individual whose hurt
but won't confront who's to blame.
It's a shame that silence can bring so much pain.
But at the same time speak
words that your actions were left to explain.

Change

Wade in the water…

My people drowned in the water.
Colonizers taking boatloads,
of priceless cargo.
These white ships are unable
to bear the weight of our black traumas.
So, the captains decided to dump
the gold into the sea leaving,
my people to suffer tragically.

Black souls left stranded
at the bottom of the Atlantic.
If you listen closely to the sea, you can hear
the voices of the gone but never forgotten.
I will never understand how these colonizers
could get rid of their treasures.
Because when they discovered my people
they struck gold.
Creating their own history,
and leaving our stories untold.

After arriving in this country,
the truth would unfold.
They realized we could overcome

the whites of America.
So, they decided to manipulate,
and confine these black pupils
to the spaces they could control.

Creating laws that would put
the negro in a chokehold.
Stripping away his family causing him
to feel like three fifths of a man.
As they would whip the pride off
a negro slaves back.
Leaving behind lashes that other slaves
could use as a roadmap to freedom.
But it's ironic how freedom
really wasn't freedom.
Slaves would run away to places separate from
the hell they lived in but still wasn't equal.
To the mother land.
This land allowed for babies to be stripped from
their mothers' hands,
and auctioned off to the highest bidder.
Like a piece of property.

This shit really bothers me!

How could one race be so cruel?
To the point where they would
decorate our necks with noose,

and rock us to sleep.
Not even care to tuck us in because
they were the ones rocking the sheets.
As they gathered around happily.
Admiring a beautiful black ornament
hanging from their lynching tree.

Negros just swaying in the air.
As the wind whistles through
the bullet holes of their bodies.
Like Emmitt who was killed and dumped
'til his body surfaced,
and his face was put on display.
Like a sculpture in a museum.

The white man's systematic structure
was placed to oppress the negro.
All because they realized my people
could soar like an eagle.
But the birds of a feather flock together,
and that Jim Crowe.
Would continue to soar to make sure
the negro was never equal.
But blacks never back down.
We stand up for our people.
Fight back like Muhammad.
Keep the chopper like Malcom.
And continue to believe
in our dreams like Martin.

Blacks were raised to have manners
so, they act civil but,
they have the right to be mad.
And want to riot electrifying
a nation like watts.
Until we receive justice,
for constant misjudgment.
And until it's presented like the laws
used to oppress my people.
There will be no peace.

We are tired of our blood being
painted on concrete.
Because you live in fear while
in our presence.
We are tired of experiencing the same thing.
We just want one thing.
Mr. Obama said it best, and that's some damn
CHANGE!

The Search for Peace

As humans we seek peace in
everything except ourselves.
On a constant search for an escape because the
world around us seems like a fire
we won't make it out of.
In hopes that some place or someone will,
come and extinguish these flames.
That have produce a smoke that's clogging our
vision and our minds like a stairwell
when the fire alarm rings.

See it's crazy that we allow our minds to be
clogged, and throw off our train of thought.
Causing us to lose track of everything in sight
as we start to derail in life,
and day by day it becomes a constant fight
to make things right.

Starting with finding peace and
instead of trying to find it elsewhere.
We must look beneath the skin and
make amends within ourselves.
Because ultimate peace comes from within
not anywhere else.

Because once that trip ends or
you done hanging out with your friends.
You're back alone again dealing with
a not so peaceful situation.
So, take some time and find peace deep within,
and once you do, you'll never search for it
anywhere else again.

Social Media

Swipe….Swipe….Swipe

People living above their means.
Just for their post to come across
someone else's screen.
Our souls are infatuated with the
comments and likes.
Willing to go to the furthest extent,
just to show the world our highlights.
Soulmates stuck in the DM's because
were too good to read them.

So…

Let's face it, the numbers on our pages entitle us
to feel like we done made it.
But those numbers won't come to the rescue,
for your life when it's time to save it.
A simple post becomes your journal
when your emotions ignite.
Leaving you wondering why everybody
is in your business.
But after a couple taps and a simple click you're
the one that put them in it.

It's crazy to think we've allowed apps

to consume our lives.
Causing the world to drown the truth
in a pool of posted lies.
So stuck on comparison we begin to lose track
of our own lives.
Posting big smiles on the gram but
you really dying inside.

In reality we bash the real because
on social media the fake is what we idolize.
Causing the real to turn fake,
just so they don't feel out of place.
Absent likes, comments, shares
and saves tend to make us feel like they hate.
But when it's the other way around
we tend to get the big head.
Talk crazy and forget to be humble because them
numbers don't mean nothing anyway.

It's comes as no surprise,
that we lose track of time.
When social media is always on our mind.
Moral of the story don't let social media
turn you into a fake and make you forget,
who you were in the first place.

As The Innocent Voices Speak

Take a second sit back and think
nowadays the average life expectancy.
Is determined by how fast a bullet
can leave the barrel of gun.
Senseless individuals playing tag with glocks
and somehow the wrong people
always seem to be it.
A series of mass shootings that
the world will never forget.

As the innocent voices speak.

Close your eyes and allow me to paint a portrait
of what innocence looks like.
As I stroke the canvas, I begin to see
a bunch of individuals in a grocery store
looking to feed their families.
As they approached the checkout little did, they
know they were about to check out due to the
deadly shells being released from aisle 4.

As I stroke some more, I see teachers teaching
lessons of "Run, Hide, and Fight". Unknowingly

prepping their students for a reality that is about
to change their life.
21 dead bodies and 17 injured which could have
been easily prevented if the police didn't hesitate
to enter.

They say a painting speaks a thousand words.
Well, this one here shouts the thoughts
of those innocent victims.
"I didn't deserve this", "I was just out having
fun with my friends", "Lord please don't let this
shooter walk in".

As the innocent voices speak.

Sometimes mass shootings are like celebrations.
The confetti rains just like bullets
over large crowds.
The cheers are like fatal shouts,
and the joyful tears flow like the bloodshed
of the innocent victims.
The only difference between the two is
the people that came with you
may not leave with you.

As the innocent voices speak.

Cheer Up

Life gets hard
Times are tough
But rainy days
Don't last forever
Cheer up

I Miss you

I have a confession to make... I miss you

It's killing me to believe that our hearts
and minds can be separate but still equal one.
It's like when you're away I can still hear your
voice in the distance like my neighbors were
playing music too loud. Anticipating an
unexpected knock at the door.
In hopes that the peep hole reveals it's you.

I promise you will never know
what I go through when you go away.
My pride tapes my mouth shut making it hard
for me to express the words my
vulnerability wants me to say.
I find it ironic that the further you are from me
physically the more I crave you mentally.

Wishing that you were here because the
memories we have in my camera roll do me no
justice.As the saying goes no justice no peace
and you're the piece,
I need to make my puzzle complete.
So bring me justice in the form of your presence
that will put me at peace.

So that I can love on you better
and I don't mean in between the sheets.

Allow me to caress your insecurities making
you feel safe in this space.
As I tongue kiss your imperfections and fall in
love with the taste of who you really are.
While simultaneously deep stroking your
aspirations as I help bring you,
to the climax of your future.
Never wanting to pull out because we do better
together, and we provide each other with
a feeling that next could never.

But I'm sorry if this seems like love letter, I just
wanted to finally remove this prideful ass tape
and tell you I miss you.

Erotic Sea

As she waves at me to come closer.
I dive deep to discover the treasures within.
The soothing touch of her
inside caresses my skin.
Leaving me soaked in the purest of waters
the world can produce.
As I lay next to her, she speaks to me
in the calmest tone I've ever heard.
Stimulating my mind as her sound becomes
therapeutic to my soul.
She lets me know that she
wants to be discovered.
And that her inner jewels are too breathless
to keep hidden within.

Truth

Is it wrong for me to seek the truth?
Because when I don't my
curiosity ignites inside.
Changing the gears in my mind to full throttle
as it speeds to the finish line
where my anxiety resides.
I don't like to be left in the dark.
But I'm patient with myself because
the truth always comes to light.

It comes as no surprise that I always sense the
hidden truth under fabricated lies.

My intuition becomes a polygraph
sending signals to my mind.
When my heart falls victim to these lies.
Leaving me thinking like maybe I'm tripping
as my soul provides me with
this torn apart feeling.

When those lies explode from your lips
It causes a war between my heart and mind.
Now I'm stuck in the middle
unable to pick a side.

Those lies cause a domino effect in my life.
Starting with the lies.
Then BOOM!
It falls into my curiosity.
Then BOOM!
It falls into my mind.
Making it hard for me to focus on
what I really need.
Then BOOM!
It falls into my anxiety causing me to stress.
Then BOOM!
It releases this lever.
That slowly drops this weight on my chest.
Making it hard for me to
Deep breath
Deep breath
Breathe.
Forcing me to count lies instead of sheep.
Constantly losing sleep,
and it's all because I do not believe.
Those words that you speak.
So, I ask of you.
PLEASE, PLEASE, PLEASE
JUST TELL ME THE TRUTH!

Genuine Bond

Have you ever grabbed a hold of someone
you didn't want to let go?
I'm talking someone so special they
penetrate your soul.
They provide you with love, smiles,
peace and joy.
A love so genuine not even the worst
of situations could destroy.
A smile so bright it could blind any
negativity in sight.
A sense of peace that you thought
only you could provide.
And a bundle of joy that makes nothing else
in this world even matter.
Even though you have never been inside.
They are similar to a door
you want to stay locked behind.
When the world seems to be attacking you,
they are where you run to hide.
The thought of them runs through your mind.
Their presence and voice sends chills
down your spine.
And when you're at your lowest you crave them
to help you feel fine.
In all hope that this bond will never end, because
like wine it gets better with time.

Is that too much to ask for?

I just want a good woman…
Is that too much to ask for?
I just want to know if you valid
like a stamp in my passport.
Like damn baby can we fly together?
Until our wings get tired,
and we land in perfect unison.
On the landing strip of perfect imperfections.
Because baby through my eyes even with your
imperfections you're still perfect to me.

I don't have to post you on my screen.
Because the world already knows.
Behind every great man is a great woman.
I'm social with you, you social with me.
And the pictures and videos we share together
are all the media we need.
Our love doesn't need to be justified by
what other people can see.

I want you to run through my mind like
the melody of my favorite song.
As my feet catch the beat captivating you
with every step in the name of love.
While our souls intertwine clearing everything

negative thought out our minds.
As we slowly journey through time until I'm
confident enough to ask will you be me mine.

Like really is that too much to ask for?

Why Lie?

They say the truth shall set you free.
So don't come to me if you can't,
handle it please.
Because the lies I've told,
have kept me shackled.
To situations I should've left a long time ago.

I understand lies comfort your emotions and
protect you from the harsh realities of life.
But I don't have time to sugarcoat anything.
The lies I could tell would seem so sweet,
to you but they feel like flames to me
that burn my tongue.
These torrid words spew from my mouth.
As they try to protect you,
from my cold heart.

That could crush your world,
and bring you down.
Like the towers on 9/11.
Because if you knew the truth
You would treat me like a terrorist.
Staying far away and being cautious,
with allowing me in your presence.

So instead of taking myself,
through the pain of keeping up with lies.
And protecting your emotions.
I'll keep it real with you.
So, I hope you can handle the truth.

Wake Up

Opportunities are hidden
In plain sight
Open your eyes
Wake up

Emotional Art

I've found a passion for expressing myself
through the form of art.
I allow my pen to illustrate images.
Showcasing my internal rage.
On these pages so that I can finally see
the beauty of my hurt.
I've struggled my whole life to express myself.
It's almost like I get stage fright when it's time
for me to shine, and say what's on my mind.
But when this pen is in my hand
it's almost like it was rehearsed.
The words slide from my mind
into the ink of the pen,
and slip right onto these pages.
Putting on a perfect performance.
As these tears flow from my eyes,
I give myself a standing ovation.
Because I was finally able to out act my fear
and allow my emotions
to put on an amazing show.

If I Had One Wish

The rest of the world wants unlimited riches like
they had Timmy Turner's wishes.
In hopes that they could take hold
of everything they envisioned.
But see me I'm different I'd be more like Ray J
and only want one wish.

That would be to bring you back
and erase that sunny day.
That forever lasts in my head
as a gloomy memory.
The one where my mama walked up to me with
tears in her eyes and said "baby yo daddy gone".
Too young to fathom everything that's going on.
But I knew one day I would have to stand up,
grow up without a father and be strong…

But let me get back to my wish.

Where I would wish just for one more chance
to start life over again.
To get to live the life I always envisioned
and that's the one with you back by my side.
Being my driver on this ride call life.

Until I'm able to take the wheel and do things
right.

In this wish you would have the opportunity
to see me excel at life and achieve everything
that you dreamed I might.
In this wish I would get to put
the biggest smile on your face.
Instead of giving the world
a remembrance of you
every time my smile shines bright.
Like your presence that brought light
to every room you stepped in.
In this wish you would be my teacher teaching
me life's lessons that no teachers could teach,
and helping me stay out of these streets.

Mr. Genie, please grant this wish for me!

Turn my dream into a reality!
So that I can hear the calming harmony
of his voice.
That would light the spark that ceased
inside me many years ago.
This wish would bring joy to me quicker
than Jimmy Johns could deliver.
But now I'm stuck here wishing because
the cops killed another nigga.
Making you the suspect and the victim.

Leaving me to learn how to be
a man on my own.
But now that I'm a man achieving everything
I could dream of.
I take some time to close my eyes and ask.

Mr. Genie, can you please grant this one wish
for me?

Goodbye Anxiety

There at times where my anxiety
weighs down on me.
So, in attempt to cure this feeling
I tune out the world
with a little Marvin Gaye Sexual Healing.
Singing a long attempting to hit high notes that
will catapult this anxious feeling out my soul.
Vibing to the melody of Bobby Womack.
I remind my anxiety it's time to
hit the road, Jack.
As it walks across 110th St.
Leaving me behind feeling very special.

Letting Go

Holding on feels great,
but letting go will feel even better.
Letting go may come with heartbreaks,
and learned mistakes.
But in the end, it's all a process to
make you better.
I've had to learn to let go of people
so that new ones can enter.
Even let go of my old ways so that new
opportunities could be presented.
It's all about facing the fear of change,
and everything that comes with it.
Without letting go you'll never
have room for more.
So, when new opportunities come
knocking at the door.
Be sure the old isn't present anymore.

Sweet Dreams

I wonder at times do dreams really come true?

I put all my hard work and time on the line,
for dream that may not even really be mine.
Like the things I envision almost
seem like wishes.
That make me feel good like receiving
hugs and kisses.
Until those wishes remain nonexistent,
and I continue with this hopeless feeling.

Thinking to myself like,
what should I do different?
While simultaneously thinking
of a way to touch these millions.
At times it seems like
me plus dreaming equals failure.
So, I've reached the point where I've stopped
dreaming and started working.
Because nothing comes to a dreamer
but more and more rest.
So, I was determined to start working
until I achieve my best.

Using my capabilities as a GPS and
opportunities as my ending destination.
I've learned to move in silence because loose
lips sink ships, and on the cruise,
I don't have time for no Titanic shit.
So I begin to maneuver around the icebergs
in the sea of life.
Continuing to keep pushing with
no clear destination in sight.

Eventually I slowly opened my eyes to realize
that, I and not a dream
is the captain of my life.

Black Man

Dear black man . . .

Allow those tears to roll off your face.
Like the words "I'm okay" roll of your tongue.
Allow your emotions to be expressed as you
tuck in your nonchalant ways
and put them to rest.
Black man allow yourself to be vulnerable
and be who you really are.
Allow your mind to be the bulletproof vest that
protects you from the bullets of judgment.
Allow yourself to discover new things that
your masculinity kept hidden.

Black man be present in your child's life
because those presents aren't enough.
Allow time well spent to fill your child's heart
with love and joy.
Allow your child to be themselves instead
of living through them to fill a void.
Black man stop making excuses and accept
responsibility for your own actions.
Allow yourself to remove those shackles
of childhood trauma.
Allow yourself to change instead

of being stuck in your old ways.

Black man you don't have to carry
the weight of the world on your shoulders.
Allow yourself to set boundaries so that weight
of others doesn't crush the little you
that you have left.
Allow yourself to say no you don't always
have to be a hero.
Black man the rest of the world is here for you.
Allow yourself to seek help, you don't have to
go through struggles alone.
Allow your mind to be free as you allow those
demons inside to move on.

Black man it's okay to work a 9 to 5
these streets really don't love you.
Allow your future to escape
an early grave or a cold cage.
Allow your knowledge to take you to that corner
office instead of the corner on the block.
Black man protect yourself at all times this
world is filled with evil.
Allow yourself to be aware that the police
protect and kill people.
Allow yourself to be the shield
in your family's fights.

Black man educated yourself refuse

to be ignorant.
Allow your mind to be the most powerful
weapon you ever possess.
Allow books to become a part of your life rather
than another inanimate object.
Black man I speak to you from one to another.
To let you know you are not alone.
You can be different than what society expects
you to be.

Ignited Soul

Burning inside is a fire in my heart
I try to extinguish it with alcohol and drugs.
But in reality, all I need is a hug.
Depression creeps in and drives me insane.
Pretending to be okay is the dangerous game
that I play with myself.
To make the world think that I'm okay.
A simple smile used to mask the pain that carries
the rage through my veins.

I had visions of big dreams.
That later became shackled by reality chains.
Unable to escape I gave up fighting
and day by day I witnessed the same stuff
I was never enough.
I struggled with my past that made it harder for
the gifts of my future to ever get opened up.

Prayers to God to help me see a brighter day.
Because every day I asked myself,
should I take my life away?
Thinking that maybe things will be
better in the afterlife.
Or maybe I'll get more recognition from the
world

once I'm a memory, and their physical presence
can no longer come near to me.

Thinking day by day should I continue
to climb this rope called life.
Or should I let go and take the easy way out?
Leaving my loved ones behind with so many
questions and doubts.
Someone please help me out!
At the the top of my lungs,
I shout but no one hears me.
Constantly in fear of expressing myself because
I refuse to let anyone experience how dark my
reality is once they come near me.

At times I feel like that old wooden chair
on the front porch.
Everyone loves to take a seat and
place their weight on me.
But what they don't realize is they
are slowly breaking me.
Until I reach that point where that fire inside
is too much to handle.
Then I finally break down
and it takes my life away from me.

Have you ever died inside but you were still
living?
Feeling like a dead battery in the back

of a clock that's still ticking.
It's a feeling that leaves me constantly
reminiscing because as life goes on,
I begin to feel like a memory.
Yet I continue to shout but
still no one is hearing me.
I just hope that when it's all said and done that
the world remembers me.

CPSIA information can be obtained
at www.ICGtesting.com
Printed in the USA
BVHW051735060623
665489BV00016BA/1118